PLATE K12　　　　　　　　　GERTRUDE STEIN　*Picasso*　The Metropolitan Museum of Art

RAIN IN THE JUNGLE   *Henri Rousseau*

PLATE K11

PLATE K9   THE VISION AFTER THE SERMON—JACOB WRESTLING WITH THE ANGEL   *Gauguin*   The National Gallery of Scotland, Edinburgh

PLATE K8   THE MOON AND THE EARTH   *Gauguin*   The Museum of Modern Art, New York, Lillie P. Bliss Collection

PLATE K7   L'ARLÉSIENNE   *Van Gogh*   The Metropolitan Museum of Art

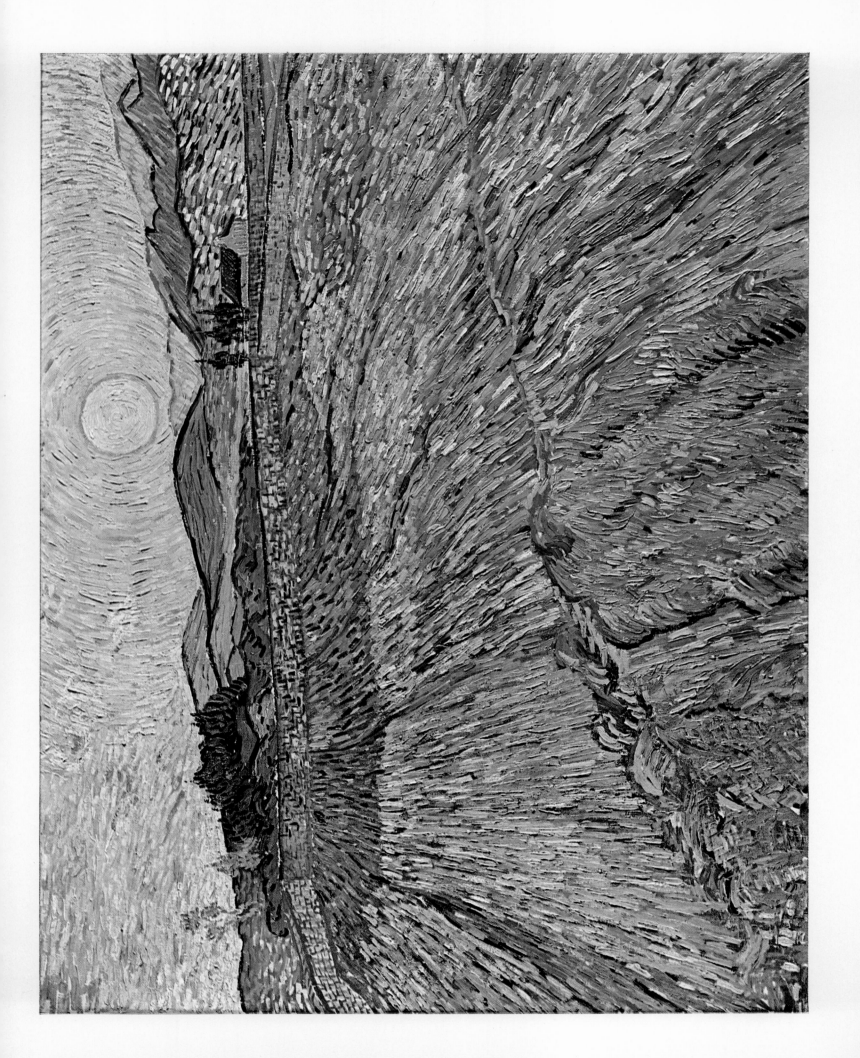

Van Gogh

LANDSCAPE WITH PLOUGHED FIELDS

PLATE K6

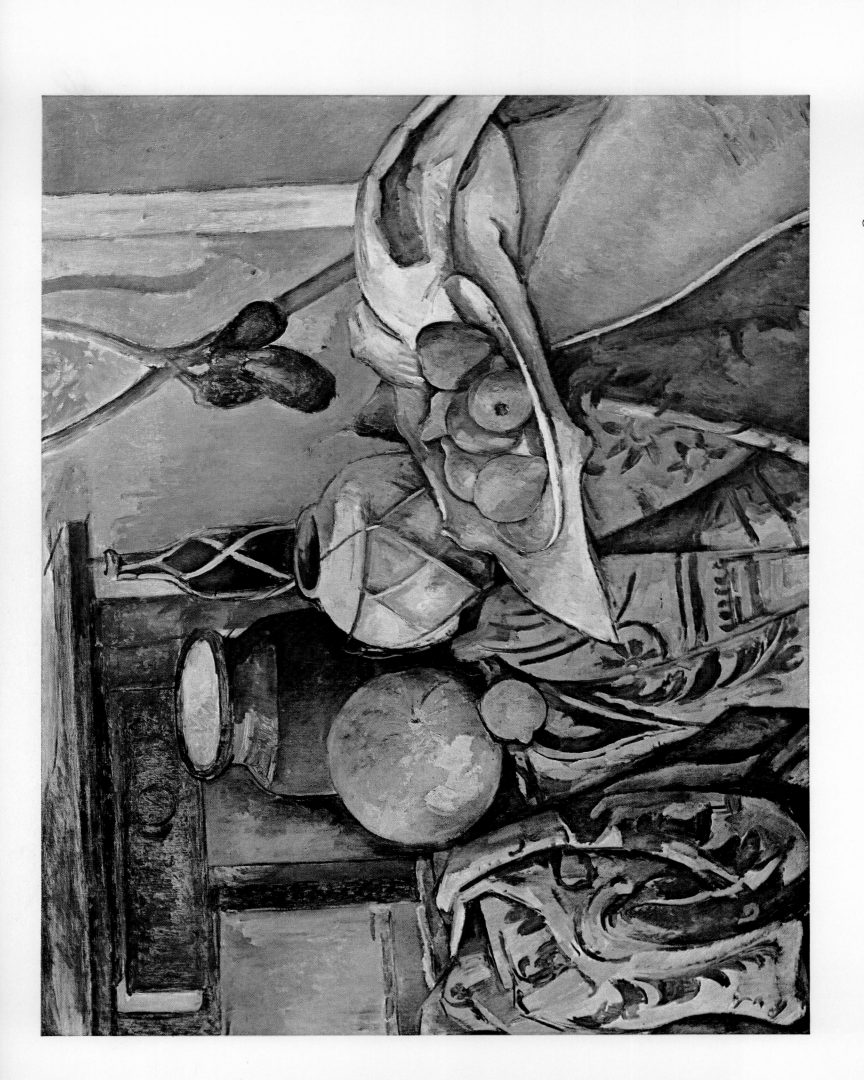

PLATE K4

MADAME CÉZANNE   *Cézanne*   Mr. and Mrs. John L. Loeb, New York

THE POOR FISHERMAN   *Puvis de Chavannes*   The Louvre Museum, Paris

PORTFOLIO K

METROPOLITAN SEMINARS IN ART

Great Periods in Painting

PORTFOLIO K

Painting in Transition: PRECURSORS OF MODERN ART

BY JOHN CANADAY

ART EDITOR AND CRITIC
THE NEW YORK TIMES

THE METROPOLITAN MUSEUM OF ART

PAINTING IN TRANSITION

Precursors of Modern Art

THE EIGHTH and last impressionist group show, in 1886, was organized after more than the usual amount of dissension. None of the shows had been easy to put together, for their goals were half idealistic and half practical. Idealistically, the members were devoted to giving new art a showing; practically, the new artists hoped for favorable attention and sales. There had always been arguments over the inclusion of this or that painter nominated by one or another of the members. Degas was especially stubborn when his nominees were objected to. Since Degas, along with Mary Cassatt and Berthe Morisot, was one of the few members who could underwrite the projects financially, he usually got his way.

Berthe Morisot, we may remember, was Manet's sister-in-law. Manet had always refused to participate in the shows. He had died in 1883, but his brother continued to be interested through his wife Berthe. When the 1886 show was proposed the brother was altogether opposed to the inclusion of a very large canvas by a young painter named Georges Seurat (1859–1891). Seurat had so far departed from impressionism that his work was something of a proclamation against it. But Pissarro argued that the canvas should be shown under the auspices of this organization that had always stood for the artist's right to paint as he pleased. At that time Pissarro himself was painting in the manner of Seurat.

Finally the exhibition was held with the works of Seurat, Pissarro, and their associates hung in a separate room. Even so, Renoir and Monet refused to exhibit. The show was an oddly mixed selection demonstrating that although impressionism had triumphed it had also yielded its place as the newest art to more recent developments. The great impressionists were forming the outer defenses of the Old Guard. The men who succeeded them as the avant-garde are now lumped under the term postimpressionists, for lack of a better term to cover their various ways of working. Among these artists Seurat and his adherents were closest to the impressionist tradition and to acknowledge their debt to the now outmoded rebels adopted the name neoimpressionists.

Seurat's canvas, *A Sunday Afternoon on the Island of La Grande Jatte* (*Figure 1*; Portfolio 7, Plate 84), caused the most trouble at the exhibition. A detail in color (Plate K 1) brings us close to the extraordinary surface of this painting.

Seurat was at work on the *Grande Jatte* while Renoir was painting the *Bathers*. In his reaction to the formlessness of impressionism Renoir had returned to a traditional way of painting; Seurat was attacking the problem by perfecting a new technique. He was covering his sixty-seven and a half square feet of canvas with dot after dot after dot of color, as laboriously as if constructing his images with pasted confetti. The colors were those of impressionism, the spectrum of red, orange, yellow, green, blue, and violet; but the application of

dots had nothing to do with impressionistic freedom. It was as scientific as Seurat could make it. After calculating the proportionate quantities of spectrum colors in the various areas of his picture he applied dots of uniform size within sharply defined areas. Impressionism's frothy mixture of iridescent tints was subjected to a catalyst that transformed it into geometric crystals.

The ingredients of impressionism in the *Grande Jatte* are two: first, the use of broken color and, second, the reference to daily life as subject matter. But both ingredients are transformed to such an extent that the impressionist connection is negligible except as a historical point of departure. The surface of the *Grande Jatte* is vibrant, twinkling here and there (it has been called "a molecular dance"), but whatever effect of light and atmosphere this vibrance carries with it is more suggestive of a controlled laboratory experiment than of nature with its freedom, its accidents, and its

informality. The strollers and loungers on this island in the Seine are carefully regulated in their pace, in their intervals of distance from one another; they carry their canes and parasols at precisely the angles dictated by a studied interrelationship of lines and shapes that includes each cane and parasol, each tree trunk, each shadow or distant curving sail. Nominally we are in the world of Paris of the 1880s, but we are closer to the timeless world of Poussin who in his *Funeral of Phocion* (Portfolio 7, Plate 76) disposed figures against an imagined classical background no more carefully, and no more artificially, than Seurat disposes them within a familiar park.

Seurat believed that perfection in painting could be achieved by subjugating spontaneous, intuitive responses to rules. He was without question the most systematic painter who ever lived. In his extreme regard for rule he may even chill us; we are forced to watch the scientist at work before we may enjoy the artist.

His scientific preoccupation went beyond theories of color. Interested in discovering a mathematical basis for pictorial composition, he investigated a formula called the "golden section," or "divine proportion," or "gate of harmony," which had been devised by the architect Vitruvius in the first century B.C. and revived in the Renaissance. In 1509 a Bolognese monk named Luca Pacioli published a book on his theory of harmonic proportions that was illustrated by Leonardo da Vinci who, as we saw in diagraming *The Last Supper* (Portfolio 6, Plate 61, *Figures 1, 2*), had made his own investigation of mathematical composition. The theory seems workable, and it is practiced by some artists today. But, like other systematic theories used in creating art, it works as well as a test when applied to much mediocre or bad art as it does for much good. In the end, the creative sensitivity and intelligence of the artist determines the effectiveness of the rules he uses, and so it was with Seurat. The exquisite compositional adjustments in the *Grande Jatte* may have their scientific or semiscientific foundations, but they are regulated by the intuitional sense and the training of a painter who, like Poussin, was creating an abstract pattern of forms to satisfy an ideal of harmony, quiet, and unity. It is necessary to make this point at such emphatic length because we must always keep it in mind as a qualifying factor when we describe Seurat's systematic way of working.

Seurat's Theories

Once his composition was determined in its main outlines, Seurat set about reducing its elements to silhouettes in accord with their basic geometrical equivalents, as we can see in a study (*Figure 2*) for the woman fishing at the far left in the *Grande Jatte*. He drew in black crayon on grained paper, taking care that the grain would show enough to suggest the divisionist sparkle of painting. (Divisionism, we should say here, is the breaking up of color into its component hues; the term overlaps another—pointillism—which is the application of color in dots of uniform size. Chromo-luminarism is a rather awkward term covering both approaches.) Then came the labor of adjustment and readjustment of composition and individual forms in study after study, until finally the labor of applying dots of paint could begin on the basis of color calculations already worked out.

Seurat tried to discover laws governing our psychological reactions to line and color and to codify them as definitely as scientists had codified physical laws. He wrote of warm dominants and cool dominants, expressive respectively of gaiety and activity or of melancholy and quiet; of lines ascending above the horizontal or descending below it, expressive of the same opposites; of the psychological effect of twisting lines or straight ones, and so on. Actually there was nothing new in any of this; the rules had been observed without formulation for centuries and

Figure 2

7

Figure 3

were not far removed from principles belabored by the academicians. But Seurat's codification was inevitably a part of his effort to regulate the totality of painting by a formula including physical laws, technique, and aesthetics.

With the *Grande Jatte* Seurat set about the task of working out a series of problems in pictures that would illustrate his theories in all possible combinations of subject and light. The *Grande Jatte* is an outdoor subject with stationary figures in full daylight. He next painted *La Parade* (*Figure 3*), also with stationary figures, also out of doors, but illuminated by artificial light. *La Parade*, sometimes translated as *The Come-On*, shows a side-show barker and musicians inveigling customers who are lined up in the foreground. The lotuslike shapes along the upper part of the composition are gas flares. The third problem in this series of subjects was a composition of three nude models, again station

ary, in a studio—but this time indoors in a natural light.

Presumably the series would eventually have included a subject of static figures indoors in artificial light; however Seurat then shifted to kinetic subjects with a picture of dancers called *Le Chahut* and followed it with *The Circus* (*Figure 4*). *The Circus* was not quite complete when Seurat died, at only thirty-two. It is generally conceded that he was weakened by the grinding hours of sheer manual labor required to execute his paintings.

By all Seurat's theories *The Circus* should be a successful picture, but it is a disappointing one. The swirling lines, by theory, express action. The silhouettes are designed to move upward in a way that should express gaiety. The color, dominated by oranges, reds, and yellows, conforms to Seurat's recipe for action and cheerfulness. But the picture doesn't work. All the ingredients are present, but rule has triumphed in a frozen image. We need only compare this version of a circus with one by Toulouse-Lautrec (*Figure 5*) to see how a more flexible—and probably only half-analyzed—application of the same general principles has brought us a circus, while Seurat has been able only to offer us a diagram of one.

Signac

Neoimpressionism, as a form of creation by recipe, attracted a large number of followers. The number disturbed Seurat, who felt that the followers were parasitic on the theories he developed with such pain. One exception was Pissarro, in his neoimpressionist phase; the great exception was Paul Signac (1863–1935), who had as much to do with the origins of neoimpressionism as Seurat did. He summarized the doctrine of the school in a book, *From Eugène Delacroix to Neo-Impressionism*, published in 1889, and after Seurat's death he continued as its leading practitioner.

Signac has his own hallmark as a neoimpressionist; a verve, a spontaneity never quite fettered by the demands of formula that bound Seurat so tightly. Signac's *Quay at Clichy* (*Figure 6*), even in black and white, is filled with his special vivacity; the dots of color are like sparks in the sky, like a fall of luminous matter on the street and sidewalk. The effect is not that of Seurat's perfectly ordered performance, and for that reason the technique employed is more obtrusive and out of key with the happy, relaxed spirit of the picture. Signac is at his best in water color (*Figure 7*), where he adopted a distinctive technique attuned to this mood. Sketching with quick, short, curling lines, spotting a few washes of clear color here and there, leaving large areas of paper untouched to set off the liveliness of his pencil and the freshness of his tints, he continued the happy spirit of impressionism at its most idyllic.

Signac has another importance in connection with an institution called the Salon des Indépendants. In 1884, two years before the last impressionist show, several hundred artists who had been rejected from that year's Salon formed a society to hold annual no-jury Salons in competition with the official one. Thus the idea that had germinated twenty-one years earlier with the Salon des Refusés finally matured. The new society was pledged to no cause other than the right of any artist to exhibit free of censorship, but naturally it represented the avant-garde who were regularly refused elsewhere. Seurat and Signac were both leaders in organizing it, and both were hard workers in getting together its exhibitions. It was while Seurat was helping to arrange the Salon des Indépendants of 1891 that he died.

Signac became president of the society in 1908 and held the position for twenty-six years. Meanwhile, similar organizations pledged to the cause of modern art appeared in other countries. An early offshoot was Les Vingt, in Brussels, with which Pissarro, Signac, and Seurat exhibited, and a spectacular single example was a Salon of sorts called the Armory Show, held in New York in 1913, which brought the modern art of Europe to America —an explosion that shattered the foundations of conservatism in the United States.

Seurat and Tradition

The revolutions that affected painting in the last century had roots in tradition. In retrospect we see them as continuations as well as departures. This is especially true of Seurat's work. The title of Signac's book *From Eugène Delacroix to Neo-Impressionism* is enough to remind us that Delacroix's freeing of color, upon which the impressionists built, is one link of a chain in which Seurat's color theories are another. And Delacroix, of course, would not have painted as he did without Rubens's example. The backward tracing can be continued link by link until it is lost in the past.

Yet the metaphor of a chain is not a very good one, since it suggests too simple a progression. An artist inherits from many sources,

Figure 4

10

and if Seurat's color makes him a logical descendant of Delacroix, his drawing, his composition, and his insistence on rule tie him much more closely to the tradition of Ingres, the adversary of Delacroix the great romantic. An artist is not so much a link in a chain as he is part of a web; while Seurat was studying Delacroix's color he was enrolled as a student under a painter named Lehmann, a disciple of Ingres, whose veneration for classical disciplines seemed extreme even to his colleagues. As Ingres had advised Degas to do, Seurat was drawing "lines, many lines," with Ingres as his model.

Seurat had another source of classical inspiration in Pierre Cécile Puvis de Chavannes (1824-1898) who at this time, in his sixties, was the dean of mural painters and a pillar of the official Salon, some rejections of his early work having been forgotten. His *Autumn* (*Figure 8*), as a typical example of his classical-decorative style, may seem a bit stuffy and

routine today, but it recalls Ingres and foretells Seurat. The nude at the right is not much more than a particularly well-studied bit of academic figure painting, simplified and clarified in accord with decorative conventions. But the central standing figure with the long straight line from hand to hip along the right side, and the neat arc of the hip and thigh on the left, plus the arc of the half-raised arm in a line that curves and then straightens into the one on the right, is designed with an eye for geometrical pattern that explains Seurat's attraction to Puvis.

Puvis remained sympathetic to innovators even at the height of his conventional success, and on Salon juries he irritated other members by the freedom of his judgments. The originality and discipline of his work is less apparent to us today than it was to young men like Seurat, simply because Seurat and others who built on Puvis make him look old-fashioned. The others included Toulouse-Lautrec, oddly

Figure 5

11

enough, who was interested in any well-drawn line although he was indifferent to Puvis's ideal of classical repose. This ideal did interest Seurat, to such an extent that he made a copy of Puvis's *The Poor Fisherman* (Plate K 2) just before he began work on the *Grande Jatte*.

When we say that an artist is part of a web, we may here see how many threads are intermingled. *The Poor Fisherman* is directly influenced by Japanese prints, another evidence of Puvis's alertness to fresh concepts even in his academic milieu. Millet's sympathetic interest in humble people and his device of ennobling them by playing their figures in solitary eminence against landscape are presented in new form. The landscape is reduced to a harmonious combination of silhouettes in delicate but decisive balance in the way of Japanese prints. The realistic rags and tatters of the Barbizon peasants are designed ornamentally in Puvis's mural tradition. Thus the serenity of the classical ideal is served by a combination of Oriental abstraction and European realism. There is also a strong dash of nineteenth-century sentimentalism, the element among all others distasteful enough to critics today to obscure virtues in *The Poor Fisherman* that were apparent to Seurat when he saw the picture.

Seurat began the *Grande Jatte* in 1884; he had a few finishing touches to put on *The Circus* when he died in 1891. If Renoir had died at Seurat's age only *Bather with Griffon*, of the pictures we have discussed, would exist to represent him; yet in a brief seven years Seurat produced pictures that establish him as a primary force in painting. One wonders irresistibly how his art would have developed had he lived a normal life span of seventy years. He would have witnessed the various "isms" of our century—expressionism, fauvism, cubism, and surrealism among them. It is difficult to imagine him continuing his obsessive concentration in the same direction through these years. He died, indeed, virtually ignorant of the work of the man who revolu-

tionized painting more than any other during what would have been Seurat's mature years.

This man, of course, was Paul Cézanne, who at the time of Seurat's death was in his fifties, a recluse in Aix, exhibiting rarely, not much more than a name to painters who had not known him in the early days of impressionism.

Cézanne: Plastic Color

We met Cézanne as an impressionist in our last discussion; earlier (Portfolios 1, 4, and 6), we gave pertinent facts about him and, by means of individual examples, some introduction to his later work. We may limit ourselves here to some explanations of his theories, trying to avoid being too explicit on a subject involving conjecture.

Each of Cézanne's brush strokes has been analyzed and re-analyzed by writer after writer. Where two analyses contradict one another there is seldom much to choose between them, and either might have surprised Cézanne, who seems to have been less certain of exactly what he was doing than his interpreters have been. He was the opposite of Seurat, who set down his rules and then followed them. With Cézanne each brush stroke was a new hazard, part of a pictorial structure like none that had ever been built. Each painting was a preparation for the next one in which he would try to build more firmly the kind of structure he had in mind. Cézanne wrote informally about what he was doing, and there are records of his conversations with friends. But the reader should bear in mind that even while we seem to be explaining Cézanne's theories as if they were as clear as Seurat's, we must remember that Cézanne himself said that he had never fully realized his goal. With this warning we may go ahead with explanations that are general enough to be true, even if the specific examples used in illustration are based on the writer's deductions rather than on Cézanne's explanations.

Cézanne's color, like Seurat's, developed

Figure 6

from impressionism's broken tints. But Seurat kept to the idea of color as light; Cézanne was determined to achieve the identity of color with form. We have seen that *Man with a Straw Hat* is modeled in rather choppy planes, the color changing, more or less, from one plane to the next. There is nothing particularly new here; the color is realistic, but we find the same thing in Courbet and in several old masters, notably Frans Hals.

However, if we compare this head with a portrait of *Madame Cézanne* (Plate K 3) painted much later, we discover that the woman's head is blocked out in planes that shift arbitrarily into pinks, blues, and creams with only a general relationship to the natural tint of flesh. In the dress the same thing happens. The general color is plum, but if we imagine such a dress as it would appear in a color photograph, we see that Cézanne shifts

from color to color, as plane joins plane, in a way that departs from the natural look of things.

To understand what Cézanne is after we must first accept what might be called plastic color—color, that is, used to model forms in space. Certain colors appear to recede in space while others tend to advance. This is less complicated than it may sound and can be demonstrated by a single example: a spot of yellow on a sheet of blue paper appears to stand in front of the blue, since yellow is optically an advancing color and blue a receding one. But a spot of blue on a yellow sheet looks more like something seen through a hole in the paper than like something on top of it for the same reason. In general, warm colors such as yellow and orange advance; in general, cool colors such as blue and blue-green or blue-purple recede. The principle is

13

affected by dozens upon dozens of secondary considerations, such as the size of the color areas, the relative intensity of adjacent colors, and the quality of light in which they are seen. For instance, our example might not hold with a dull, impure yellow and a bright, pungent blue.

Cézanne's idea was to break objects into planes and then select for each plane a color that would make it advance or recede to the degree he wanted, bringing the near facets forward by advancing colors and pushing the far facets back by receding colors. This is an extreme oversimplification. When a painter tries to apply the theory the local color of objects presents immediate complications: how, for instance, to make a yellow lemon stay in the background when a blue vase, let us say, is in the foreground. The complications increase enormously when we remember that objects and colors next to one another modify one another. Seurat might have tried to make a working formula involving all the variables but Cézanne did not. He might ponder a brush stroke for a quarter of an hour before he was satisfied that in tint and intensity the color was the right one as part of the structure.

There is no way to analyze the artist's reason for each stroke in the head, or the dress, of the portrait of Madame Cézanne without assuming too much. We do not know how satisfied Cézanne was with the result.

Figure 7

What we can see without question is that the form is powerfully stated, wonderfully coherent and integrated, by whatever means.

We have spoken only of the head and the dress, but in a Cézanne no single area can be regarded as independent from the others. The tawny chair back, the blue wall, the dark stripe that divides the blue from the light dado below it are less complicated than the head and the dress, but they too are painted not as blank areas, but as a multitude of contiguous planes making up final broad planes of the background unified with the figure that dominates them.

Delacroix anticipated plastic color when he objected to the way David and Ingres used color as if it were a kind of dye to be washed over forms already modeled in black and white. He, too, held that form and color should be one, and he found colors within colors in his "merging of reflections." Next the impressionists developed the broken surfaces of pictures like Monet's *Île aux Fleurs* (Plate J 1). This opened the way for Cézanne to transform each broken stroke into a plane and finally, by their colors, to turn these planes toward or away from us, binding a picture together as a structure in which form and color were inseparably united, identical.

But we must insist once more that Cézanne's revolution is not necessarily complete. He made a revealing statement when he said, "I am the primitive of the way I have discovered," meaning that he had taken a step in a new direction, but far from the final step. In this way he has been compared to Giotto (Portfolio C). Giotto, too, was the primitive of the way he discovered. It was not until the appearance of Masaccio, a hundred years later, that Giotto's revolution was assimilated and enlarged upon. Our concluding discussion will show that Cézanne's revolution has affected painters in many different ways, but whether he has yet found his Masaccio is a question.

Cézanne: Formal Distortion

The concept of plastic color is only a part of Cézanne's revolution. For six hundred years before Cézanne painters had sought to re-create more or less truthfully the appearance of the visible world. They might idealize natural forms, exaggerate some aspects of them and ignore others, create fantasies based on them; but in the end they respected their proportions and their symmetries. The impressionists, we have seen, were the ultimate realists in recognizing the union between the painter's eye and his art, using the eye as a lens and the canvas as a surface to catch images in reflected light. But Cézanne rejected natural appearances; he distorted the forms of the visible world in ways and for purposes that departed from this long tradition.

Still Life (Plate K 4), painted 1890–1894, is the kind of picture that seemed to prove to many of Cézanne's contemporaries (and even to later critics) that he was incompetent by even the most rudimentary standard of draughtsmanship. And certainly by representational standards the green pot just at left of center is out of kilter. Its two sides do not match and its rim is oddly tilted, rising behind and dipping in front. The wine bottle near it stands askew. The table behind both would never satisfy the laws of perspective. A dark tone—we cannot call it a shadow—runs along the right side of the pot, clinging to its edge, and continues unreasonably along the edge of the large green melon and into a fold of the cloth. In front of the melon is a lemon; a strong, thin dark line, not even following the lemon's contour, separates the two pieces of fruit. The plate holding pears and apples looks warped; also, its back edge, at both right and left of the fruit, is hardly defined against the white cloth. Taking as our standard the sober realism of a still life by Chardin (Portfolio 2, Plate 20) these distortions are unpardonable or at best inexplicable. Yet Cézanne's concept of still life has enriched our understanding of Chardin.

The purpose of these distortions, and others that occur in the picture, is to unify the objects and the space around them in an abstract scheme that will give us greater pleasure or will hold a deeper meaning than we can find in an accurate reproduction of objects nicely arranged. The tilt of the bottle, the tilt of the table leg, and the flattened side of the green pot bind the three objects together as parts of a diagonal movement in the over-all pattern. Imagine the left side of the green pot swelling outward symmetrically with the right, and you may see that the pot would become part of a group of three rounded objects—pot, ginger jar, and melon—leaving the bottle rather too thin and tall by contrast and making the group of rounded objects a bit monotonously bulbous and overconspicuous. Distorted, the green pot is a transitional and unifying form; it shares the roundness of the objects in front of it, yet is united also with the thinner, lighter forms behind it.

The dark blue area, not quite a shadow, clinging to the right edges of pot and melon serves to flatten their mass. It also tends to pull them together in a single plane by creating a strong line defining their edges continuously, as if they were a single object instead of two separate ones. The principle is well known to painters, but the practice is ordinarily avoided as a fault. It is one of the first mistakes a beginner makes in learning to reproduce the appearance of objects. Fully aware of what he is doing, Cézanne flattens and binds his objects by the deliberate use of a device that made him seem irrational or stupid at a time when drawing and design meant representational drawing and design.

At this point the reader may still ask why it was necessary for Cézanne to flatten or pull toward a single plane objects that rightfully are fully round and in different planes. The answer is given in the first sentence two paragraphs above, but it is worth repeating because it is easy to lose sight of: Cézanne's problem is not to imitate the relationships of space and volume in the objects he has set up to paint but to create a new unity of objects and space in an abstract scheme.

The objects in a Chardin are so tangible, they occupy their own volume of space so convincingly, that we can imagine picking them up, moving them about, rearranging them— at loss to the picture's composition, no doubt, but without difficulty. But in our Cézanne it is difficult to imagine removing the melon, for instance, without leaving a hole in the picture. Cézanne said, "I do not want to reproduce nature; I want to re-create it." By reproducing nature, with slight modifications or with idealizations, the artist may emphasize this or that aspect of it—in Chardin's case, the dignity inherent in simple things. But by re-creating nature into a new scheme at once so stable and so full of life, so wonderfully integrated yet so full of variety, Cézanne assures us that the world is not only fascinating and various on its surface but controlled by inner forces of logic and order.

Cézanne's goal was to take the world as it

16

is, to relish its actuality, its impact, yet to discover the harmonies that are obscured by its complexities and accidents. Artists by the score have held the same goal, but most have solved their problems by simplification and idealization of reality. Neither solution was acceptable to Cézanne, since either involved some sacrifice, he thought, of the world's innate order and vitality. He said as much in his two most revealing statements, first that he wanted to make of impressionism something solid and durable like the art of the museums, and second that he wanted to do Poussin over again after nature.

The two statements mean almost but not quite the same thing. Conceivably he might have included, in the first, some reference to the technique of broken color, which he did make solid and durable by transforming it into a means of expressing form. Certainly he meant that he wanted to paint with an impressionist's response to the immediate world. But he also wanted to paint pictures that, like Poussin's, would be ordered in a way that assures us of life's reasonable and logical basis. Poussin's art was orderly but perhaps a bit removed and chill; impressionism was near and warm but concerned with ephemeral things. Cézanne's goal was to combine the virtues of these opposites without accepting

Figure 9

17

their limitations, and he managed to achieve it.

He insisted upon painting in the presence of his subject, as the impressionists did, drawing constant sustenance from it. His apples rotted away during weeks of work; when he painted flowers, he used artificial ones; he subjected himself to hours upon hours in the fields, day after day, painting pictures like *Landscape with Viaduct* (Plate K 5). The impressionists painted outdoors to observe natural light, but Cézanne was not interested in natural light. The light in *Landscape with Viaduct* is his typical all-pervasive, steady, and timeless light, identifiable with no specific part of the day and no specific atmospheric condition. But, feeling as he did that only in the presence of nature could he maintain communication with it, he was unwilling to risk synthesizing landscapes in the studio as Poussin did or even to re-create real landscapes from memory and sketches made on the spot as the Barbizon men did. His intense regard for nature had little to do with spontaneous lyrical response. Nature was for Cézanne a manifestation of universal order, the order of classicism made vibrant by its revelation in the commonplace.

In *Landscape with Viaduct*, as in the still life, Cézanne pulls the elements of the subject closer to the observer than they are in nature. We look from an eminence across a deep valley to the distant peak of Mont Sainte-Victoire, the low mountain near Aix that Cézanne painted over and over again. But the mystery and haze of distance are eliminated in a composition of logic and clarity. The planes of the hills are as clearly defined as the planes of the foreground foliage; hills and then fields are pulled proportionately closer to us plane by plane until the deep landscape is contracted into a closed and compact structure. Some devices similar to those described in the still life are apparent here: the dark line of the road winding through the center abuts upon the tree trunk. A realist would have softened the line (as well as lightened it in value) to make it pass behind the tree trunk. Cézanne

seems to use it as a brace for a rising form that leans slightly toward the right. The viaduct, farther in the distance, abuts upon the tree in much the same way, although less emphatically. Noticeably, its small segment to the left of the tree drops slightly in level, increasing the effect of contact between tree trunk and viaduct, calling attention to their function as parts of a structure rather than to their interest as parts of a scene.

There are two kinds of perspective in the usual landscape: linear perspective by which systems of lines converge at vanishing points and aerial perspective by which forms soften and fade in the distance. Linear perspective is hardly discernible anywhere in *Landscape with Viaduct*, and aerial perspective is minimal. The houses in the background are not quite as definite as those in the foreground, but they are far more definite than the soft, ambiguous shapes of natural vision at such distances. Cézanne's idea of perspective, as well as his concept of form, was identified with color. "Color is perspective," he said, and in talking about his work to his friends, he used to point to passages where he was dissatisfied because the color remained merely color, not simultaneously color and perspective. It happens to be true that Cézanne's pictures are magnificently ornamental in terms of color alone, a fact that accounts for much of his popularity today when his work hangs in reproduction in houses where nothing is asked of a picture but that it look well as a spot of decoration on the wall. But this ornamental richness was of very minor interest to Cézanne.

In late works Cézanne's compression of space increases to the point where Mont Sainte-Victoire and the valley around it are brought close to a single foreground plane. The small planes become increasingly abstract, until their origin as houses, bushes, fields, and roads is hardly recognizable. *Mont Sainte-Victoire*, a very late picture (Portfolio 1, Plate 8), can be placed by *Landscape with Viaduct* as a self-explanatory illustration of this.

Figure 10

The Great Bathers

Meanwhile Cézanne also occupied himself with compositions involving several figures. He was forced to synthesize these, since it was impossible to find models who would pose for the length of time required to complete a picture involving three to five people. We have commented at some length on one of these, *The Card Players* (Portfolio 6, Plate 69). We should see one other, *The Great Bathers* (*Figure 9*), since it is a key picture in modern painting.

The subject is an odd one for Cézanne, since its artificiality denies his premise that natural, unpretentious material offers the most vital connection with life. But it had interested him

for some time; he had made numerous small studies of bathers in a landscape. Now he felt impelled to attack a conventional subject on a large scale, to prove his mettle with a picture that would challenge comparison with manifestos of other painters.

The most insistently architectural of all Cézanne's works, *The Great Bathers* is constructed on a framework of three main systems. First there is the strong arch established by the several tree trunks and suggested by parts of the human figures. A countersystem, moving downward to a climax where the arms of the central figures reach toward a focal spot, reverses this upward thrust. Strong stabilizing horizontals, established by the horizon and river banks, run across the center and lower portions. Over all there is an insistent movement into compositional depth, most apparent in the figure at lower right, lying on her stomach.

Although it is heretical to do so, we might complain that the figures in this picture have been abstracted to the point where they suggest disturbingly malformed human beings but not beyond this to the point where we would have to accept them as abstract forms. In spite of this criticism, *The Great Bathers* is an impressive picture and one that, for many people, stands as the culmination of Cézanne's art.

Van Gogh

Cézanne and Seurat may be called the classicists of postimpressionism. The romantics were Vincent van Gogh (1853–1890) and Paul Gauguin (1848–1903). Van Gogh represents the nineteenth-century romantic ideal of self-release through art, of tragic vehemence, of visionary ecstasy, all demanding a way of life in which reason and order are sacrificed without compromise when they stand in the way of emotional fulfillment. Gauguin also represents this way of life, the difference being that he chose it and Van Gogh was forced by circumstance to accept it. Gauguin continued the traditional romantic search for the exotic, the strangely colored, the bizarre, the primitive, as an escape from the humdrum. He represents romantic Bohemianism; Van Gogh, not quite justly, the apotheosis of mad genius.

Van Gogh was not mad. In his last years he was subject to irrational periods accompanying epileptoid seizures. As their severity increased he was hospitalized for observation and such treatment as could be given by doctors with scant knowledge of his affliction. His suicide did not occur during an attack, however; it was apparently an almost impulsive act, committed with a revolver whose ownership has never been traced. We conjecture that the weapon was sighted by chance and borrowed from a peasant, perhaps with

the excuse that Van Gogh would shoot some of the crows that infested the fields. Yearning for love and companionship but inspiring little response to the affection he poured out so generously, unable to hold a job for long, without a market for his pictures (he sold exactly one during his lifetime), supported by his brother Theo, who could not easily afford the allowance he gave him, Van Gogh chose this desperate solution to the problems of increasing illness and the burden he felt he was imposing on others.

The story of Van Gogh's life has been a gold mine for biographers, but it is best told in his letters, particularly those he wrote Theo. They are illuminated by fraternal devotion and the joy of work that sustained him in a life that might otherwise have driven him truly mad. Because we know his terrible life we often read tragic implications into his work where they do not exist. Van Gogh's tragedy was in his frustrations, his defeats; his pictures were his release from those frustrations and are his victories. They may be all but intolerable in their intensity, but they are seldom tragic.

In *Landscape with Ploughed Fields* (Plate K 6), Van Gogh transforms gentle earth, an old stone wall, and a farmhouse and low hills in the sunlight into an expression of the pulsating energy of life. The transformation is complete. We can imagine the scene as painted by Daubigny or Corot, with the quiet fields protected by bordering walls and the small house peaceful within the confines of the hills; or as painted by Monet, a cool shimmer of reflected tints, fresh and airy; or by Cézanne, an ordered world in the manner of *Landscape with Viaduct*. Van Gogh's landscape is none of these. It lies open to the radiation of the cosmic fireball; the fields respond with a vivid growth, the hills curl and swell in its heat. Nothing is inconsequential or casual, nothing is serene or gentle. The last stroke of color is as intense as the first, and everything is defined as part of a universe whose smallest particle is charged with energy flowing from and back to

Figure 11

the sun. At times Van Gogh's landscapes writhe with the force of this energy finding release, as it does in *The Starry Night* (Portfolio 3, Plate 25). Very occasionally he finds a world that is cool and gentle. In *Rain* (*Figure 10*) we see the same fields, wall, and hills that we saw in *Landscape with Ploughed Fields*, painted here in soft grays, lavenders, blues, and pale olive greens, cut across by rain lines in these same colors. Now and then Van Gogh shows us a flowering tree or an orchard where blossoms are fresh and tender. But he always returns to a world brilliant in blazing light.

He painted the great majority of his landscapes (and his other pictures, for that matter) in southern France, many of them only a few miles from Cézanne's sites. The country was home for Cézanne, his native ground where he felt secure as he never quite did in Paris; and this feeling for the country is reflected in the solid and enduring character he gave it. But for Van Gogh, the Dutchman, the southern landscape was a revelation of warmth and strong yellow light that excited him as no other countryside had done.

Van Gogh first worked seriously at painting in depressed areas of Belgium, where he had failed disastrously in an effort to become a minister. He was interested in Millet at this time (at one time or another he seems to have admired every painter, good and bad, in his feverish questing), but he discovered that the peasant and the laborer were not so much nature's noblemen as society's victims, and he painted some dismal pictures of their dreary lives. The most ambitious of his early semi-sociological pictures was *The Potato Eaters* (*Figure 11*) of which he wrote, "I have tried to make it clear how these people, eating their potatoes under the lamplight, have dug the

21

earth with those very hands they put in the dish, and so it speaks of manual labor, and how they have honestly earned their food." Saying that he wanted to paint a "*real* peasant picture," he went on: "*I know it is*. But he who prefers to see the peasants in their Sunday best may do as he likes. I for my part am convinced I get better results by painting them in their roughness than by giving them a conventional charm." The picture's depressing color is, intentionally, suggestive of earth and potatoes; the awkwardness is in part intentional, in part the result of Van Gogh's limited experience at that time.

After he failed in his preparation for the ministry Van Gogh decided to devote all his time to painting and studied briefly at the Academy in Antwerp before gravitating to Paris. He worked for a while in a class with Lautrec, who took a compassionate interest in him. People who knew him in this delayed period of study—he was already in his middle thirties—have described an ugly, timid, fanatically earnest man who worked at his draw-

ings until he wore holes in the paper and who remained on the edges of gatherings until, unnoticed, he slipped away. But he was learning by seeing. He deepened his acquaintance with impressionism and discovered pointillism. His color lightened. When he made his first southern trip to the city of Arles in 1888 he was ready to exchange the dull oil lamp of *The Potato Eaters* for the radiant sun.

He had also discovered Japanese prints, as is apparent in the background of his portrait of Père Tanguy (*Figure 12*). Tanguy was a dealer in artists' materials and informally a dealer in pictures as unsalable as those of Van Gogh. (There were times when it was possible to see Cézannes in Paris only at Tanguy's shop.) As often as not he took pictures in exchange for materials, to the distress of his wife, who was of a practical turn of mind. He was a man whose personality combined naïveté and grandeur. Van Gogh's portrait is remarkable for its combination of these qualities, and coloristically it is a landmark in his development. The colors are strong and bright; the blue mass of the coat is surrounded by emerald greens and bright orange-yellows; everywhere there are shots of vermilion. A purely arbitrary vermilion line separates the figure from the background. When he painted the gloomy *Potato Eaters* Van Gogh said, "I am not at all anxious for everyone to like it or admire it at once." In the portrait of Père Tanguy, although he had taken a new direction, he was still painting in a way he knew would please few people and be understood by even fewer. In truth, he was anxious for approval and touchingly appreciative when it was offered, but he would work by no standards other than his own. In a man so lonely and so eager for friendship, this integrity is all the more admirable.

He formed a one-sided friendship with Gauguin, a crudely handsome, arrogant man who was successful with women where Van Gogh consistently failed. Staked by Theo, Gauguin visited Vincent in Arles, where the

Figure 13

the subtlety of oriental line is rejected for bold points, swellings, concavities, and straight edges that support and contradict one another in rapid succession. Van Gogh had thought of stained glass in painting his sunflowers; there are reminders of it in this portrait where the thickly applied paint approaches the physical character of glass and is bound here and there within dark outlines like the leading of medieval windows.

Impressionism proved remarkably varied in its offspring, with Cézanne and Van Gogh at opposite poles. Impressionism's broken color and neoimpressionism's calculated dots were the origin of the hundreds of short strokes of strong color that crowd so excitedly across *Landscape with Ploughed Fields* and whirl and twist through the cosmos in *The Starry Night*. Cézanne said "Color is perspective"; Van Gogh could have said "Color is emotion." He was the first modern expressionist (we have discussed him as such in Portfolio 3), and although he once said that he felt sure of his recognition in the future, he could hardly have believed that he would become one of the half-dozen major influences on the art of the next century.

Van Gogh worked hard at the problems he set for himself. The pictures that seem to have poured onto the canvas as if he were only the instrument of forces beyond his control were actually the result of a great deal of preliminary thought and study. His development was staggeringly rapid. With the exception of early, groping efforts like *The Potato Eaters*, his life work covers a period of but two years. His suicide occurred only eighteen months after his first arrival in the south, yet in that short time he realized himself. His last months were spent in Auvers-sur-Oise, where he went to be near the benign Pissarro (who would have taken him into his home if his wife had not objected to so eccentric an influence on the household) and a Dr. Paul Gachet (himself rather eccentric) who kept him under observation.

two men painted together. In anticipation, Van Gogh decorated the house with a series of brilliantly ornamental pictures, among them the painting of the sunflowers of Arles, violently yellow against pale green (*Figure 13*). The sunflower paintings are popular today in thousands of reproductions, although even the best of these are pallid and insignificant compared with the enamel-like brilliance and large scale of the originals.

Both Gauguin and Van Gogh did portraits of a Madame Ginoux, a neighbor who posed in regional costume. (Both portraits are commonly called *L'Arlésienne,* or *The Woman of Arles.*) For his background Van Gogh used the pure, singing yellow that now obsessed him, playing strong blues and purples in front of it (Plate K 7). Unlike the portrait of Père Tanguy, this is not a projection of the personality of the model; rather it is an expression of the power that Van Gogh, who had known only the soft light of the north, now felt in the southern sun. The influence of Japanese prints is carried into the flat, silhouetted shapes, but

Gauguin

By the time he made his visit to Van Gogh in Arles, Gauguin was an impoverished man. Not many years before he had been a successful broker, but he abandoned his business and his family to lead a life whose story may be read either as one of sacrifice to a creative ideal or as one of renunciation of responsibility. In his relationships with people, including Van Gogh, whose adulation he accepted and callously exploited, Gauguin behaved reprehensibly. His flouting of bourgeois standards included on one hand some clownish exhibitionism. On the other, he suffered and died as a painter whose dedication to his art was as constant as his love of self-display.

From the first, exoticism was part of his life. He was born in Peru. During his days of vagabondage he was briefly a digger on the canal in Panama. An early visit to Martinique so impressed him that he was led eventually to the South Seas. There he settled, a Parisian Bohemian surrounded by a richly exotic variation on Rousseau's ideal of the "natural man," embodied in beautiful, half-naked people moving within a landscape of palm trees and flowers.

But there was another aspect to this paradise. The colonial officials were narrow, pettifogging, and corrupt. Gauguin loathed them, quarreled with them, and lived in isolated spots to avoid them. The natives were beautiful, but they were also infected with diseases contributed by the Europeans who usurped their islands. The idea of wild fruit to be had for the reaching up and picking was attractive in theory; in practice it was misery when, without money for food, Gauguin subsisted on mangoes for weeks at a time. Sun, sea, mountains, and mild climate were insufficient to offset the debilitation of an ailment that caused him, Gauguin recorded, to spit a liter of blood a day. A grass hut in a tropical grove makes a pretty picture, but it is a dreary place to die, as Gauguin did, alone and untended, with a suppurating leg.

In some pictures Gauguin shows the islanders as they appeared in their daily activities, in others in westernized dress (*Figure 14*). In still others he translates their easy grace into attitudes of rigid formality borrowed from Egyptian, Indian, or other Eastern sculpture and painting, as he does in *Ia Orana Maria* (Portfolio 4, Plate 48), a tapestrylike composition on the Christian theme of Madonna and Child adapted with great sophistication to a primitive locale. But the theme that most interested Gauguin was that of the superstition governing the feelings of primitive people for whom the spirits of the dead, of the earth, of storm, of sky, of evil, and of protection were real and omnipresent.

To create visual images of this haunted world, Gauguin took elements from its tradition and added them to the amalgam of his own style. The unlikely union of the tradition of Ingres and the forms of savage idols produced such hybrid offspring as *The Moon and the Earth* (Plate K 8). Like Seurat, Gauguin was an admirer of Puvis's patterns, and if his moon goddess is not at first connectable with the classical Diana, she has her parentage on one side in Puvis's patterned allegorical female nudes. Hence, genealogically, Gauguin's moon goddess is the granddaughter of Ingres's little goddess of the spring in *La Source* (*Figure 15*). For all their dissimilarities, *La Source* and *The Moon and the Earth* could hang side by side without too much disharmony. Degas, who worshiped Ingres, liked *The Moon and the Earth* enough to buy it.

Gauguin's South Seas paintings are adaptations of material that to the European eye is inevitably charged with mysterious associations. But even before he left France for the tropical islands Gauguin was interested in primitive beliefs in the supernatural; and during a stay in Brittany he had dealt with such matters in much less obvious subjects. These earlier canvases lack the appeal of the exotic

25

and of Gauguin's fully developed decorative manner, but they are rewarding especially because they do explore material that was less ready-made than the island subjects.

One of the most powerful of them is *The Vision after the Sermon* (Plate K 9) in which Gauguin pictures Jacob wrestling with the angel, in literal terms as he imagined it might have appeared to a group of Breton peasant women returning home from church, their minds filled with the Sunday sermon. Gauguin's problem was to invest the picture with

an air of the supernatural without pretending to paint a picture of faith; that is, as a sophisticate, to stand outside a subject of miraculous and visionary nature, yet to create the miraculous and visionary experience of the faithful peasants. His solution was to take the shapes of reality and pattern them in ways sufficiently curious to suggest that they were aspects of another realm. The regional costumes of the women, particularly their bonnets, offered a starting point for flat patterns bizarre enough to carry this suggestion. All the other shapes in the picture are oddly warped to the same effect. Realistically represented, as they had been by dozens of genre painters for Salon consumption, the costumed women in a Brittany meadow would have been merely picturesque. Their vision might have been represented, again realistically, in a halo of light in the usual way, making a standard storytelling picture of the Salon type. The well-known picture by Jules Bastien-Lepage (1848–1884) of Joan of Arc hearing the voices (*Figure 16*) was approached in this realistic narrative way, although with an unusual degree of sensibility. For Gauguin this was not enough. Bastien-Lepage tells the story in sound, conventional prose; Gauguin tells it in poetry of a new meter invented to create mood rather than to describe an event.

The color in *Joan of Arc* is realistic, although modified into a harmony closer and more quiet than nature's. The color in *The Vision after the Sermon* is strong and unnatural, or antinatural. The field where the struggle takes place is bright, solid red, at exactly the opposite pole of the spectrum from grass green and thus at maximum removal from reality. Color so used is, like Van Gogh's, expressionistic. But here it has another, prophetic function. Quite aside from the mood it creates, the color in *The Vision after the Sermon* is an arbitrary pattern in itself. The red field must be red, not green or yellow or purple, because red belongs there as part of a color composition independent of expressive or realistic

Braun & Cie, New York   *Figure 15*

Figure 16

values. Thus Gauguin anticipates the color structure of fauvism, one of the several modern "isms" that we will soon examine.

Fantasy

Superlatives are dangerous, but if any is permissible, we can say that, of all times, the end of the nineteenth century in France was most richly and variously productive in painting. When we remember that Monet, Degas, Renoir, and the other impressionists were in their full powers as mature artists, when we add Seurat, Cézanne, Van Gogh, and Gauguin

as we have just seen them, when we remind ourselves that the Salon painters, headed by Bouguereau and Gérôme, were still going full tilt—a superlative is already admissible. Even within these groups we have had to omit others like the Symbolists, associated with Gauguin, and the Nabis, a group of colorists connected with both impressionism and early forms of expressionism. Then there are the dozens of painters of great interest who have become obscured by their more dramatic and investigative contemporaries. One of them is the academician Gustave Moreau (1826–1898), whose *Oedipus and the Sphinx* (Plate K 10)

27

Figure 17

shows how the linear tradition of Ingres and the colorist one of Delacroix could be combined in the art of a sound workman who was original without being an innovator. Moreau's heavy debt to his predecessors is direct, obvious, and frankly admitted, but he is his own man all the same, a fantasist whose lushly painted versions of mythological and Biblical episodes have less to do with ancient Greece and the Bible than with an other world of his own imagining. As a teacher in the École des Beaux Arts Moreau was a staunch defender of academic disciplines. Like Puvis de Chavannes, however, he encouraged dissenters (among them Matisse) when he recognized qualities in their work that warranted their dissatisfaction with conventional training.

In an unobtrusive way fantasy pervaded art at the end of the century. And as fantasy should do, it found expression through painters whose private worlds offered them subjects or interpretations beyond schools or formulas. In Moreau it forced its way against the dead hand of academicism. In Odilon Redon (1840–1916) it took more expected form, often tied to literary associations and marked by the blurred character thought of as typically dreamlike (*Figure 17*); in Henri Rousseau (1844–1910) it proclaimed itself triumphantly in pictures by an untrained amateur. A minor customs official—he was nicknamed Le Douanier, or the customs collector—Rousseau led a mildly eccentric but pleasant life as a neighborhood character in an undistinguished lower bourgeois quarter of Paris. He was a Sunday painter, as Gauguin was at the beginning. But instead of throwing everything else over for his painting, as Gauguin did, Rousseau continued in his little routine until retirement. A small pension gave him a minimum living, and the minimum was enough for him. Without passion, but with great satisfaction, he continued to paint. He exhibited in the Salon des Independants and received steadily more attention. He was a freak among painters, if you wish, since there had never been one quite like him (he has had many imitators since), but he was a benign freak and undeniably a painter with a kind of genius.

His genius seems to have stated itself imperatively, and by surprise, over the amateurish surface of his early work. In pictures like *Landscape with Cattle* (Portfolio 12, Plate 142) his effort was directed toward a precise, decorative realism. It resulted in enchantment. Other painters became interested in him; following their advice he avoided formal training and cultivated his own primitivism as a style. This contradiction in terms, and in spirit, "cultivated primitivism," could have been offensive. It is offensive as an affectation that is frequently met today. But Rousseau possessed a charmed talent. Without leaving Paris (although he claimed to be recalling experiences in Mexico, which may or may not have had some foundation in fact) he fabricated jungle scenes and poetic fantasies like *The Sleeping Gypsy* (Portfolio 12, *Figure 18*) where his piquant combination of innocence and sophistication takes us intimately into what must be called a logically aberrant world.

Rain in the Jungle (Plate K 11) is in Rousseau's late style, with the knifelike edges of its patterns, its assurance of design, its insistence upon absolute statement, as if the painter's world of fantasy were present around him for examination and accurate recording. We believe Rousseau's fantasies because he leaves us no room for doubt. Surrealist painters, not long after, were to combine Rousseau's paradox with Freudian theory in some of the more spectacular novelties of the twentieth century.

The Early Picasso

When Cézanne died in 1906, the two men who were to dominate the complicated developments in art during the first half of the new century were at decisive stages in their development. Henri Matisse (1869–1954) was thirty-

Figure 18

Figure 19

seven years old; we will see him as the leader of fauvism. Pablo Picasso (born in 1881) was twenty-five and at the point of transformation from gentle, charming romanticism to cubism.

Picasso, a Spaniard, had been something of a child prodigy, running through academic training in his country, then shifting briefly to a form of impressionism. Gravitating naturally to Paris, he was at first strongly influenced by Toulouse-Lautrec. Then, in the first of his independent styles (specialists divide his career into as many as eighty periods), he adopted the emaciated and angular forms of his "blue" period. A typical example, *The Old Guitarist* (*Figure 18*), painted in a color scheme of cold blues and blue-greens, is obviously descended on one side from El Greco. It is also related to the nervous and elongated forms of Roman-

29

esque sculpture, like those we saw in the tympanum of Vézelay (Portfolio B, *Figures 3, 4*).

The pathetic mood of *The Old Guitarist* is a little forced, a matter of adopted style rather than of deep feeling in the work of an inventive, ambitious, and vigorous young man. Picasso soon abandoned the mood for the lighter one of the "rose" period and its subdivisions. Instead of starveling guitarists he painted such delightful and gracious figures as *Boy Leading a Horse* (*Figure 19*), a full-size study for a magnum opus, *The Watering Place*, that was to have shown boys leading and riding horses to and from a pool. But Picasso's ideas were growing too fast for him to get them all set down on canvas; *The Watering Place* never got beyond preliminary compositional sketches on a small scale and studies for its parts. A new enthusiasm for Cézanne, plus Picasso's discovery of African sculpture, put the "rose" period behind him as an interval of youthful charm, to be succeeded by the torrent of his mature work.

Picasso (and Matisse) were part of the circle surrounding the American expatriate, experimental writer, and patroness of experimental art, Gertrude Stein. Picasso's mountainous portrait of her (Plate K 12) was going well except for the head. Returning to the studio one day for a sitting, Miss Stein found the head scraped out and repainted as we see it now, a sharply defined and simplified mask influenced by those from primitive Africa (*Figure 20*). She is said to have objected that it did not look like her; Picasso is supposed to have replied that that made no difference, since if she lived with it long enough she would come to look like it. The picture does look like Gertrude Stein; even more, it sug-

Figure 20

gests her Parnassian presence in those years. But likeness aside, it marks the end of Picasso's interest in appealing stylization and the beginning of the formal inventions that, from now on, will serve him in his experimental ranging from intellectual abstraction to violent emotionalism. To this point Picasso belongs with the men we have been discussing here—the precursors of modern art. Beyond this point, he is the titan of the twentieth century.

Color Plates

Figures in the Text